CW00369844

LITTLE BOOK OF
TAKE THAT

LITTLE BOOK OF
TAKE THAT

First published in the UK in 2007

© G2 Entertainment Limited 2014

www.G2ent.co.uk

Printed and bound in Europe

ISBN 978-1-782812-47-0

Contents

06   The Take That Phenomenon

22   Forming The Perfect Boy Band

26   Take That's Svengali – Nigel Martin-Smith

30   The Years Of Success 1992 – 1996

38   Robbie Williams

50   Gary Barlow

58   Mark Owen

64   Howard Donald

70   Jason Orange

76   Robbie's Departure & The Break-up

82   For The Record: The TV Documentary

90   Greatest Hits

96   The Autumn Tour 2007

102   Never Forget – The Stage Musical

106   And Robbie Makes Five

114   The Singles

128   The Albums

The Take That
Phenomenon

RIGHT
Take That
were originally
put together
to be the UK's
answer to New
Kids on the Block

Gary Barlow, Howard Donald, Jason Orange, Mark Owen and Robbie Williams each possess, in their separate ways, unquestioned talents. When these talents were merged together in 1990 under the banner of Take That, the mixture became explosive. And in the new century, after the echoes of this explosion had all but died away, the first four of these got back together to show that the old charge remained. When the fifth finally rejoined in 2010, they showed it was still possible to relight the old fire.

To scale the heights that Take That did in their first coming is almost unprecedented. To leave the stage for ten years and then return to achieve equivalent success is truly phenomenal, especially when conventional wisdom dictates that boy bands who have acquired a teenage girl audience rarely, if ever, maintain their appeal. Their fans retain a little sentiment, sure, but do they still go on record-buying sprees as they did before? Not as a rule.

Because, it has to be admitted, the singers in the band had set the bar incredibly high for themselves. Selling more than twenty million records in the first half of the 1990s was a colossal achievement. Their albums (*Everything Changes*, *Nobody Else* and *Greatest Hits*) all made it to the Number 1 spot, with the sole exception of their debut *Take That And Party*, which went to Number 2. Take That also had eight chart-topping singles, the first four going straight to the top in succession, a feat not achieved since those heady days of the 1960s when the Beatles were in their pomp.

As for their concert appearances, they had provoked a brand of hysteria

LEFT The re-formed Take That, with their Brit Award, 2007

THE TAKE THAT PHENOMENON

RIGHT
Robbie's bad
ways were not
always the right
image for a boy
band

similar to Beatlemania. It was during their shows that the couple of years the band spent honing their craft in the hard-to-please discos and gay bars bore fruit. They had learned how to whip up a storm with almost every type of audience, and were able to maintain their professionalism, in the midst of scenes of wild enthusiasm, to thrilling effect.

What was the Take That thrill founded upon? Like most good formulas, it was an essentially simple one. The group was unashamedly based on a desire to entertain. A potent blend of Hi-NRG disco foot-stompers and crowd-pleasing light rockers provided the excitement while the soaring ballads drove arrows straight to the hearts of their following. Every song aimed to stimulate the primary emotions, and the band members became masters at hitting the right spot.

Such success always exerts a price. Strains within the group began to show. Manager Nigel Martin-Smith had notoriously imposed a regime of almost monastic seclusion upon the young superstars. No girlfriends were allowed, drugs were completely forbidden and some of the highest

earners in showbiz were confined to receiving spending money of £150 each week. Admittedly, the group found some of these restrictions easy enough to evade, and there were quite a few stories in the press of wild nights that didn't always involve supermodels and Robbie. Nevertheless, they were, to a greater or lesser extent, chafing at the bit and it seemed to be getting some of them down.

Robbie Williams was the first to let the pressures affect him badly. His behaviour grew more erratic and his utterances more divisive. A much-publicised binge with the members of Oasis at the Glastonbury Festival in 1995 proved to be the straw that broke the camel's back. It became a question of whether he'd leave before he was pushed. A press conference on 17 July 1995 announced that he was no longer in the band.

It was the beginning of the end. Although the four remaining members soldiered on as successfully as before, the magic had somehow gone. Rumours of an impending split were consistently denied, but another press conference, on 13 February 1996, confirmed that

THE TAKE THAT PHENOMENON

RIGHT
Robbie was
hitting the self-
destruct button
with his binge
drinking

FAR RIGHT
The band shortly
after Robbie
departed

they were true. Emergency hotlines were set up to deal with the frenzied calls of distraught fans. One more chart-topping single and an album of greatest hits and the group had gone.

The critics predicted great things for all the five original members of the band, but curiously it was only Robbie, who had jumped ship first, who fulfilled these expectations. His solo career has been wondrously successful; a battery of great songs, backed by an ever-present willingness to explore and confront his demons, makes him consistently fascinating to the public. Maybe it was because he was, at least superficially, the one happiest in the spotlight.

By contrast, Gary, the main songwriter, began with two Number 1 solo singles, but gradually withdrew from public gaze, partly due to critical reaction, until it seemed he was content to be a power behind the scenes, concentrating on his writing. It was not quite the meteoric ascent people assumed he would make.

Similarly, Mark started with a couple of Top 3 singles, but also faded from public consciousness – until he won *Celebrity Big Brother* in 2002. Jason

RIGHT The four members of Take That announce their Ultimate Tour, 2006

GARY BARLOW

MARK

THE TAKE THAT PHENOMENON

tell the story. Surprisingly, everyone, including Robbie, agreed to take part. Less surprisingly, people agreed that, if there was an audience for a TV show, there might also be a market for another album release.

The Ultimate Collection – Never Forget was released in November 2005 to mark the ten years since the band split up. Not many albums can boast such a roster of Number 1 singles, with the exception of Take That's *Greatest Hits* of which this was a virtual repackaging. *Today I've Found You*, an aptly-named track from the archives (earmarked originally as a follow-up to *Back For Good*) was the only addition.

Otherwise the hits rolled back the years: *How Deep Is Your Love*, *Never Forget*, *Back For Good*, *Sure*, *Love Ain't Here Anymore*, *Everything Changes*, *Babe*, *Relight My Fire*, *Pray*, *Why Can't I Wake Up With You*, *Could It Be Magic*, *A Million Love Songs*, *I Found Heaven*, *It Only Takes A Minute*, *Once You've Tasted Love*, *Promises*, *Do What You Like* and *Love Ain't Here Anymore* (US version) with the new song at the end. It reversed the order of their hits and, one more time, Take That struck a

took up acting for a while but felt unfulfilled and Howard became a DJ with a growing reputation in England and on continental Europe. And there it seemed the amazing story might end.

But anniversaries are very important in the showbiz world. As a decade since the group imploded drew to a close, there was talk of a TV documentary to

£7
Binuculars

£15
Pink Trucker Cap

£10
Programme

£15
Blk Beanie Hat

£4
Keyring

£3
Jason Photo Card

£3
Mark Photo Card

£3
Howard Photo Card

£3
Gary Photo Card

£4

£5

£7
Mug

chord with the record-buying public. The album peaked at Number 2. So far, so good.

Such was the spontaneous outpouring of emotion released by the ending of the ten-year wait that a tour seemed the next logical step. Gary, Howard, Jason and Mark indicated they were up for it.

The tour was a sell-out and the

ABOVE
Merchandise from the Ultimate Tour in 2006

THE TAKE THAT PHENOMENON

RIGHT
Take That's
opening night in
Newcastle, 2006

group did not disappoint their eager audiences. Although the boyband had become a manband in the intervening years, the response was no less enthusiastic for being more considered. It was (almost) just like the old days.

On 9 May 2006, the group signed a deal with Polydor. This time around, all the members of the group (and even some outsiders) assisted in the songwriting. There were more rumours that Robbie might return, but no dice. The first single, *Patience*, released at the end of November 2006, shot to Number 1 and was voted the Best British Single of 2006 at the Brit Awards. The *Beautiful World* album was lauded by the critics, and it was followed in 2008 by *The Circus* and a string of hit singles.

Then, in 2010, the longed-for full reunion happened. Robbie announced in July that he was rejoining the band, and there was to be a new album, *Progress*, and a stadium tour. *Progress*, in fact, became the fastest-selling album of the century and the tour has obliterated box office records.

With the tour due to end in the summer of 2011, this is where the story stands today. Yet where did it begin?

Forming the
Perfect Boy Band

In 1990, Manchester was at the heart of the UK's music scene. Wherever one went, the Manchester sound with its novel mixture of reggae, dance and rock was predominant. Bands such as the Stone Roses, Happy Mondays, Inspiral Carpets and Charlatans were the names on the lips of music fans. But for one man in the Manchester entertainment industry, it was not enough.

Nigel Martin-Smith had noticed that, although record sales for these bands were reasonable enough, they were not massive. To achieve that level, he reckoned, any group would have to have crossover potential, avoiding the increasingly narrow definitions into which the music business was falling. In short, for a group to be staggeringly successful, it had to be a pure pop group.

With the appeal of Bros starting to fade, there was only one such group around at that time. New Kids on the Block had been the first boy band import from the USA since the teenybop days of the Osmonds and David Cassidy in the early 1970s. They had just had two Number 1 hit singles in the UK with *You Got It (The Right Stuff)* and *Hangin' Tough*. A British version, and in particular a Manchester version, was called for, reasoned Martin-Smith.

This conclusion happened to chime in with his background. Martin-Smith was a showbiz man. He had cut his teeth in the casting side of the entertainment business, and he set about fulfilling his vision in the way he knew best. He began to cast the parts of the boys in the band.

The first essentials were to have a sensitive singer and an extremely good-looking one. Fortunately he had the pair on his books under the name of the Cutest Rush. The sensitive singer-songwriter was Gary Barlow, who had been playing in clubs for several years already. While recording at Manchester's Strawberry Studios, he had met Mark Owen, a former child model and Manchester United triallist, who was working there as a teaboy. The two got on well and formed a duo, singing Gary's songs and a few covers.

Some good movers were also vital to the band's success. Jason Orange and Howard Donald were both dancers who admired each other's styles and had formed the dance duo Streetbeat. When they approached Martin-Smith, he put them together with Gary and Mark. The nucleus of the band was formed.

But there was one other ingredient crucial to making it all go with a zing – a cheeky chappie – and this time there wasn't one on tap. Advertisements were duly placed in the trade magazines. Robbie Williams had been a child actor (whose biggest role had aptly been the Artful Dodger in *Oliver*), and he attended the auditions after his mother had spotted the advertisement. Everybody immediately knew he was

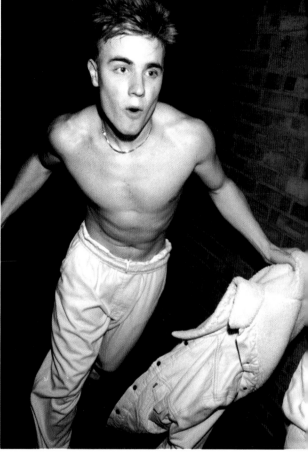

right, and he got the part.

However, beyond casting, there was no blueprint for chart domination.

For a start, there wasn't even a name. Various ideas were put forward, and at one time it looked as if the group were about to be called Kick It. Fortunately, this was ditched and they settled on Take That, apparently inspired by an article on Madonna, then at the height of her powers and her establishment-baiting fame. What all parties were agreed on was that they wanted to be a pure pop band.

Next they had to address the problem of building up a fan base. Teenage girls (and younger) were an obvious target audience, but the teen magazines proved surprisingly resistant to the group at first. So Martin-Smith had to fall back on known ground and the band began to build a reputation in the gay clubs and bars. It certainly helped that they were all natural performers (in Gary's case, with a storehouse of experience) but nevertheless it was a tough training ground.

So, too, were the schools and under-18 clubs where the group sweated to broaden their appeal. However, the hard work eventually began to pay off. The band had been noticed and they were signed to RCA Records in 1991.

Any hopes that the group were about to become an overnight sensation soon stalled. The first single, *Do What You Like*, despite (or because of) famously being hyped by a video of the ever-willing members of the band rolling around in jelly, inched into the Top 100.

As the guys admit, there was no masterplan behind their career; they just tried out different things to see if they worked. Martin-Smith was not a long-serving music business professional (like, say, Pete Waterman, whose influence was at its peak in the late 1980s and early 1990s) but a showbiz enthusiast.

He had had a clear vision of the group he wanted to see, and had cast them superbly, but had no real yardsticks by which to develop their potential.

The next single, *Promises*, did marginally better, reaching Number 38 in its two-week spell in the charts in November 1991. The third, *Once You've Tasted Love*, lasted a week longer, but peaked at Number 47 in February 1992. It was a case of one step forward, one step back. Obviously the group had something but they didn't seem quite able to express it on record – or at least the public had yet to take the bait. It's arguable whether today's harassed music business executives, driven by corporate demands and the instant expectations of reality shows, would have kept faith for so long.

It was the release of a cover version of the old Tavares hit *It Only Takes A Minute* that unlocked the door. Staying in the charts for eight weeks, it rose as high as Number 7. This was even higher than previous versions – by Jonathan King in 1976 and Tavares in 1986 – had reached and there was collective joy and relief all round.

The breakthrough was at hand.

LEFT to right, Mark Owen, Howard Donald, Jason Orange, Robbie Williams and Gary Barlow

Take That's Svengali – Nigel Martin-Smith

Every pop sensation has to have a Svengali behind them. It's part of the unwritten lore. Think of Elvis Presley and Colonel Tom Parker, remember the Beatles and Brian Epstein. For a brief period, Andrew Loog Oldham inspired the early Rolling Stones, while Tam Paton controversially did the same for the Bay City Rollers. More recently, there have been Simon Fuller and the Spice Girls, matched by Louis Walsh and Boyzone. Nigel Martin-Smith was the Svengali behind Take That.

Born in 1958, Nigel began his career in the early 1980s as a casting agent for theatre, film, television and commercials, based in Manchester's Royal Exchange. He came to believe strongly that the showbiz industry was too focused upon London and that the North West could more than punch its weight in the entertainment field. He was determined to prove his point.

In 1989, he branched out into pop music management, signing up Damian and releasing a version of *The Time Warp* from *The Rocky Horror Picture Show*. Damian had had two earlier stabs at the charts in 1987 and 1988 with *The Time Warp*, grazing the lower reaches each time. Now, with a remixed version, the song went to Number 7 and stayed in the hit parade for thirteen weeks. Nigel is quite proud of the fact that the song still gets played today … although Damian only scored one further Top 50 success with an update of *Wig Wam Bam*, the 1972 smash for glam rockers The Sweet.

Toe dipped in the water, Nigel now took the chance to prove that Manchester could offer the world a genuine pop boy band and worked hard to put Gary, Mark, Howard, Jason and Robbie together. He then drove them around the UK to gigs, jammed into his Ford Escort. With hindsight, the black leather and studs approach might have been a little rough for a teenage audience, but he learned fast. He didn't really have the in-depth music business experience to handle Take That's career faultlessly, but he did possess a great deal of savvy and enthusiasm, which more than made up for it once their bandwagon had taken off. The results he achieved as their manager speak for themselves.

It's fair to say that Nigel's methods and personality have always divided opinion sharply. At one time, during Take That's glory years in the first half of the 1990s, he was lauded as the most influential gay person in the music industry. Robbie Williams was rather less charitable in his assessment, and others undoubtedly found him a controlling figure. But it is undeniable that his vision and effort were instrumental in putting the group together.

When Take That split up, he secured a consultancy deal with Virgin

TAKE THAT'S SVENGALI – NIGEL MARTIN-SMITH

Records and managed the relaunch of Lulu's career, having already given her substantial support when she was invited to sing with Take That on their Number 1 *Relight My Fire* (incidentally, despite winning the Eurovision Song Contest with *Boom Bang-a-Bang*, and covering David Bowie's *The Man Who Sold The World*, Lulu's first and only chart-topper).

He also managed the pop career of Kavana, the stage name of actor Anthony Kavanagh, who left the TV series *Coronation Street* in order to release two albums, *Kavana* (1997) and *Instinct* (1999). There were also several singles, notably *Crazy Chance* (written by Howard Donald), a Number 16 hit in 1997, and *MFEO* and *I Can Make You Feel Good*, which both went to Number 8 the same year.

Similarly, Nigel managed the transition of former child model and actor Adam Rickitt from *Coronation Street* to pop stardom. Adam's first single, *I Breathe Again*, went to Number 5 in the charts, but follow-up singles *Everything My Heart Desires* and *Best Thing* were less successful, as was the album *Good Times*.

In 2005, Nigel was invited to contribute to the TV documentary *Take That – For The Record* as co-producer, and stayed to manage the relaunch of the band's career via the repackaging of their *Ultimate Collection* album and the subsequent sell-out national tour. On the eve of the tour, it was announced the band had once more parted company with their former Svengali, amid media speculation that such a parting of the ways was opening the door for Robbie Williams to be welcomed back into the fold. And so it has come to pass.

Nigel is generous in his praise of his one-time charges. "I can't believe what a success the comeback has been," he said after the reunion. "I thought they would do the tour and that would be it. But now they could tour every year and pack stadiums."

These days, Nigel divides his time between many business interests, under the umbrella of NMSM. The company has offices in Nemesis House, Bishopsgate, Manchester, from where the Nigel Martin-Smith Management Company continues to seek out new pop music talent.

There are four other companies run by NMSM. Lime Actors perhaps represents the closest to Nigel's roots in the business, being a management company for professionally trained actors. By contrast, Urban Talent is an agency that looks to discover real people who might turn out to have a natural talent for television. Smith's is a high-fashion model agency that specialises in work at the glamorous end of the spectrum, while Nemesis Models is a model agency that deals with commercial and photographic models at the less rarefied end of the market.

Furthermore, he is the owner of three successful enterprises on Canal Street, the centre of Manchester's gay nightlife 'Village'. The New Essential is the latest incarnation of the Essential nightclub, which closed in 2010 and re-emerged as Klub Mancunia, only to be relaunched in the autumn under its new name. Queer is a daytime café-bar that metamorphoses into a club-style bar by night, and Glam is a revamped, "pink" version of the Falcon men's bar. In this way, he manages to keep his finger on the pulse of a core interest group.

The Years Of Success 1992–1996

RIGHT A visit to New York for the band, who sadly have never conquered America

By the end of the summer of 1992, the Take That bandwagon was really starting to roll. In August, the album *Take That And Party* was released and peaked at Number 2 in the charts. As well as the singles that had helped to build the group's reputation (*Do What You Like*, *Promises*, *Once You've Tasted Love* and *It Only Takes A Minute*), three further tracks went on to enjoy success in the UK charts. *I Found Heaven* was released to coincide with the launch of the album and reached a respectable if slightly disappointing Number 15 slot.

It was the next three singles that confirmed Take That were here to stay. First, *A Million Love Songs* came out in October and rose to Number 7, equalling the band's breakthrough success with *It Only Takes A Minute*. Then, crucially, *Could It Be Magic* was released just before Christmas and became the band's first Top 5 success, peaking at Number 3 and remaining in the charts for twelve weeks.

Could It Be Magic continued the group's tradition of highly energised cover versions. Written by Barry Manilow, it had been a Top 30 success for him in the UK fourteen years earlier, and, two years before that, a Top 40 hit for the female whirlwind Donna Summer. When *Why Can't I Wake Up With You* was released in February 1993, it peaked agonisingly close to the top spot, resting at Number 2. In addition, the album also contained the title track, *Satisfied*, *I Can Make It*, *Never Want To Let You Go* and *Give Good Feeling*. The nation was partying.

The first major tour to promote this album cemented the group's reputation. On twelve successive days in November

2002, Take That played Newcastle, Bradford, Cambridge, London, Bristol, Portsmouth, Wolverhampton, Manchester, Derby, Scarborough, Manchester again and York. The concerts were a triumph. Only one thing was missing.

But the first coveted Number 1 hit record was only a whisper away. When *Pray* came out in July, it raced to the top, and was followed there with dizzying speed by *Relight My Fire* (featuring Lulu) in October, *Babe* as the Christmas single and *Everything Changes* in April 1994. Not since the days of the Beatles had a band released four consecutive chart-toppers. Now Take That definitively ruled the singles market, although the spell was fractionally broken when *Love Ain't Here Anymore* only reached Number 3 in July.

Meanwhile, the group played nine rapturously received summer concerts at Manchester, Glasgow, Manchester (again), Birmingham, four nights at Wembley (including an Extravaganza) and the Chelmsford Spectacular.

There could be no gainsaying the group's overall staggering success. The album *Everything Changes* had raced

to Number 1 when it was released in October 1993. Bolstering the six mighty singles (*Why Can't I Wake Up With You* was given another airing) were *Wasting My Time*, *If This Is Love*, *Whatever You Do To Me*, *Meaning Of Love*, *You Are The One*, *Another Crack In My Heart* and *Broken Your Heart*.

The Everything Changes tour was Take That's biggest yet. Before Christmas 1993, the group took in three nights at Bournemouth, Cardiff, three at Birmingham, Belfast, Dublin, Brighton, three at Wembley and Manchester, Sheffield, two at Glasgow, Aberdeen and Whitley Bay, provoking widespread pandemonium.

Afterwards, they swept through Europe with two nights in Rotterdam and Brussels, three in Berlin, Kiel, two in Munich, Zurich, two in Dortmund and Frankfurt, Helsinki, Stuttgart, Vienna, two in Milan, Bologna and ending with two in Rome.

Before summer 1994 was over, the group had blitzed these islands again. They played four gigs in Glasgow, three in Manchester, two in Dublin, five in Sheffield, two in Cardiff, nine at Wembley and in Birmingham,

LEFT Another 'Nineties' awards dinner

concluding a punishing tour with two in Belfast.

The rushing vortex of tour, album, tour, album raced on. *Sure* was released as a single in October 1994 and confidently took the Number 1 position. There was a slight gap before *Back For Good* (a song with erroneous intimations of longevity if Take That fans were reading the runes) followed it there in April 1995. Finally, *Never Forget* came out in August, by which time the band had been reduced to a foursome.

It was exhausting and it couldn't last. Tempers started to fray within the band, and there were many arguments between band members and the manager. In particular, Robbie Williams and Nigel Martin-Smith were constantly at loggerheads, with Williams chafing at what he considered to be the excessive control placed on the musicians. He flirted very publicly with the Gallagher brothers, Noel and Liam, the founders of another Manchester band, Oasis, making it very clear he preferred the indie rock 'n' roll lifestyle. He left.

Meanwhile, the third album, *Nobody Else*, had also powered to the top of the charts. As well as the three singles and the title track, listings included *Every Guy, Sunday To Saturday, Hanging On To Your Love, Holding Back The Tears, Hate It, Lady Tonight* and *The Day After Tomorrow*.

The Nobody Else tour consisted of ten concerts in Manchester and ten at Earl's Court, before the group headed for Adelaide, Melbourne, Sydney,

Brisbane and Perth, two nights in Bangkok and Singapore, two in Tokyo and wrapping up in Djakarta.

Rumours were circulating that the remaining members of the band had had enough of life in the goldfish bowl. Fans couldn't believe it, and were temporarily relieved when a press

FAR LEFT
The band toured enormously, including Japan

LEFT The group met Princess Diana at the 'Concert of Hope' AIDS benefit in 1994

THE YEARS OF SUCCESS 1992–1996

BELOW Robbie
Williams pictured
shortly after his
departure

conference was called for 13 February 1996. Surely these stories would now be quashed? But the rumours were true and the break-up was announced with immediate effect.

"We're all a bit nervous," explained Gary, "so if we don't have the answers to your questions we do apologise. Can we just say thanks for everyone's support over the last five years. You've been absolutely fantastic – but unfortunately, the rumours are true … as from today, there's no more. Thank you."

There was only time for a final single, the affecting 1977 Bee Gees song *How Deep Is Your Love*, released the following month, and a chapter-ending Greatest Hits collection which came out in May. Both single and album naturally hurtled to Number 1. Take That were sticking to the great showbiz adage – "always leave the crowd wanting more". But it did seem that it was the end of a fantastic journey.

BELOW Robbie Williams pictured shortly after his departure

LEFT Gary Barlow and Howard Donald briefly re-unite, at the 'Party in the Park', 1998

Robbie Williams

After he left Take That in 1995, Robbie Williams sold more albums in the UK than any other British solo artist in history – with sales over fifty-seven million worldwide. With his singles estimated to have sold around sixteen million around the world, his total sales to date are well over seventy million. This is an incredible achievement for the boy from Stoke-on-Trent who began his career with one of the most phenomenal bands of all time.

Born Robert Peter Williams on 13 February 1974, Robbie has simply had one of the most exciting careers of any solo artist in the history of music. His talents don't just include pop – which is where he first found his niche – but comprise a variety of musical styles from adult contemporary to dance, swing, rock and rap. Time and time again, Robbie has proved to those who doubted that he could make it big time on his own, that he has got what it takes. Continually reinventing himself, Robbie entered the *Guinness Book Of Records* in 2006 when

tickets for his world tour went on sale. More than 1.6 million tickets sold in just one day.

So what makes this performer such a super star? Well, he's talented, has sex appeal and constantly performs what millions of fans want. He's enthusiastic on stage and interacts with his audience in a way that's personal – he comes across as if he's singing for a whole bunch of mates, rather than a paying crowd.

Between 1998 and 2007, Robbie was the world's best-selling male artist with eighteen million albums and six million singles sold in the UK alone. The only performer to have more Number 1 albums than him is the legendary 'King' of rock 'n' roll, Elvis Presley. In 2010 he received the Outstanding Contribution to British Music award at the BRIT Awards. Including his time as a member of Take That, the megastar has sold in excess of a hundred million albums, singles and DVDs worldwide since his career began in 1990.

Despite his iconic status, Robbie

LEFT Robbie
was seen as the
joker of the band

ROBBIE WILLIAMS

hasn't always enjoyed the good life. Soon after leaving Take That he battled with drugs and alcohol and was often seen in public looking dirty and dishevelled. He has also had weight problems, which led to Noel Gallagher of Oasis referring to Robbie as "That fat dancer from Take That" at Glastonbury in 1995. For his part, Robbie had painted a tooth black and dyed his hair peroxide for the event. His reputation in the media wasn't good at the time and many were cynical about his abilities to pursue a solo career.

After sorting himself out and treating himself to a decent shampoo, Robbie was back in 1996 and ready to launch his solo career. His first single was a cover version of the George Michael/Wham! song *Freedom*, which climbed to Number 2, but Robbie still needed to clean up his act and went through rehab for drug addiction before releasing a second single.

That turned out to be *Old Before I Die* – a Number 2 in 1997 – taken from a debut album (*Life Thru A Lens*) that spawned five singles which would see Robbie heading for the sky. Next came *Lazy Days* and *South Of The Border*, which reached Number 8 and 14 respectively, but it was the fourth single

harvested from the album that began Robbie-mania.

The emotive *Angels* – voted the best British song of the previous 25 years at the 2005 Brit Awards and the one that most people would want played at their funeral – saw the light of day just before Christmas 1997 and peaked at Number 4. It had been claimed that Robbie was sounding too much like an Oasis clone but *Angels* reversed the public's perception of him and began the love affair that continues to this day. The single has sold more than six million copies worldwide.

Released in March 1998, *Let Me Entertain You* reached Number 3 and Robbie was looking more and more like a success story. But he was finding it hard to break through on the other side of the Atlantic even though in the UK and the rest of Europe he was consistently storming the charts.

I've Been Expecting You was awaited eagerly, and when it was released in 1998 Robbie didn't disappoint: the album sailed merrily to the hot spot in the charts, going on to sell 2.7 million copies in the UK alone. The first single chosen for release was *Millennium*, which gave

him his first UK chart-topper as a solo artist. It was followed by two Number 4 hits in *No Regrets* and *Strong* before the double A-side of *She's The One/It's Only Us* returned him to the top of the charts. (His first two albums were combined and released in the States as *The Ego Has Landed*.)

Rock DJ from the third album, *Sing When You're Winning*, had moderate success in the US but the controversial song took Robbie all the way to Number 1 in the UK in 2000. The song itself wasn't the controversial bit; that came with the video, in which Robbie strips nude among a horde of female fans. Using CGI technology, the singer is then seen 'stripping' off his skin, muscle tissue and organs, which he feeds to the ravenous fans. The skeleton of Robbie dances to the music until the end of the track. It was nominated for an MTV Video Music Award, but the nudity and violence led to a negative public reaction.

He returned to Number 1 in the UK with *Eternity/The Road To Mandalay* in 2001, the same year *Swing When You're Winning* – an album of cover versions of songs from the 1950s and 1960s – was released. It is an exciting album that

LEFT Robbie has always been a great performer

BELOW Robbie on stage in 2000

shows off the true extent of the talents of Robbie's voice. Sounding exactly like a crooner from the age of swing, he manages to replicate jazz, blues and pop styles of that time. *Somethin' Stupid* (a cover of Frank and Nancy Sinatra's original duet) with Nicole Kidman became a Number 1 Christmas hit in the UK.

The follow-up album, *Escapology*, released in 2002, received mixed reviews. Although the album took Robbie back to a pop-based style, he was still struggling to make a breakthrough in the US. The video for the album's second single, *Come Undone,* did nothing to enhance Robbie's reputation: it depicted the singer having three-way sex with two women, although he remained fully clothed. The album saw his long-term partnership with writing partner Guy Chambers come to an end.

The following year saw Robbie playing three consecutive nights at Knebworth in front of a total of 375,000 fans. These events confirmed his status as the most popular solo artist in the country and the album *Live At Knebworth*, released in October 2003, has gone on to sell around four million copies worldwide.

A *Greatest Hits* compilation was released in 2004 and debuted at Number 1, with more than 320,000 copies flying over retailers' counters in the first week alone. It included two new songs, *Radio* and *Misunderstood*, the former giving him his sixth UK chart-topper.

Intensive Care came next, three years after its studio predecessor, with a highly publicised worldwide launch in October 2005. Having partly given up on the US, Robbie announced that the album would not be launched in North America. He changed his mind when demand was high for his latest music and it was released on iTunes on both sides of the Atlantic. It went to Number 1 in the UK and sold an amazing 373,000 copies in its first week, and with worldwide sales reaching the six million mark it is the singer's fastest-sellingalbum. *Sin Sin Sin*, the fourth single released from the album, gave Williams his first taste of life outside the Top 20 when it charted at Number 22 in the UK.

Mixed reviews greeted *Rudebox*, featuring collaborations with Joey Negro, the Pet Shop Boys and William Orbit among others, in 2006. The album's title track received a damning review from

The Sun, which named it "the worst song ever", but it did give him his highest US hit to date at Number 19. Gary Barlow felt it wasn't Robbie at his best. He stated that he liked: "Classic Robbie Williams … and this isn't classic …" To date, *Rudebox* is his lowest-selling album.

The 'comeback' album was 2009's *Reality Killed the Video Star*, recorded with producer par excellence Trevor Horn and featuring one song co-written with Guy Chambers. The album has been a big

LEFT The Live 8 concert in 2005. Robbie performed amongst a host of stars

BELOW Robbie on stage, 2006

ROBBIE WILLIAMS

RIGHT
Robbie in
his element, as
he performs to a
capacity crowd

global seller, despite being beaten to the UK Number 1 spot by the debut of boy band JLS.

Next out of the Williams locker was another greatest hits compilation, *In and Out of Consciousness*, and it included a Robbie–Gary Barlow single, *Shame*, that was a result of the reunion with his Take That mates.

The Robbie bandwagon kept rolling in 2012 with the release of his ninth studio album, Take the Crown, which was received warmly by the critics and yielded a number one hit single in Candy. The following year saw him continue his love affair with swing, first revealed in 2001 in Swing When You're Winning, with the album Swings Both Ways. The first single from the album, Go Gentle, reached the UK top ten and the album put Robbie on a par with Elvis Presley as the joint-second maker of the most number of UK number one albums.

Despite his enormous success, Robbie still finds life difficult at times. Known to suffer from depression, insecurity and self-loathing, he is loved and adored by millions of fans worldwide. It is a shame that this exceptional performer finds it so difficult to love himself.

Gary Barlow

With a curriculum vitae that includes sixteen self-penned hit singles during the 1990s, Gary Barlow is surely one of the most talented songwriters of these times. That claim was backed in 2009, when he was voted Britain's greatest songwriter, beating John Lennon and Paul McCartney into second and third places.

Born on 20 January 1971 in Frodsham, Cheshire, the songwriter, singer, pianist and producer entered the BBC's *Pebble Mill At One* 1986 A Song For Christmas competition with *Let's Pray For Christmas*. As a result of making it to the semi-finals, Barlow was invited to record his song in London aged just fifteen.

Inspired and enthusiastic, the young singer decided to try his luck on the northern club circuit with a mix of his own material and cover versions. In 1990 he took on Barry Woolley as his manager but soon came to the attention of Nigel Martin-Smith and became the lead singer of Take That. He was forced to settle out of court with Woolley when his former manager threatened to sue him.

Gary was the first Take That member to launch a solo career. His 1997 release *Forever Love* stormed up the charts and gave the singer his first Number 1 single. The album *Open Road* also made it to the top spot and he claimed his second Number 1 single with *Love Won't Wait*. Unlike former bandmate Robbie Williams, Gary made it to the charts in the US with *So Help Me Girl* and this was followed by a second album, *Twelve Months, Eleven Days*, in 1999.

Party In The Park, hosted by London's Capital Radio in Hyde Park, featured Gary in both 1998 and 1999. He had been dubbed the greatest songwriter of the 1990s, but the media were ruthless and turned their backs on him at the end of the decade when Robbie began to excel in his own solo career.

Robbie's *Angels* was the song that turned the critics against Gary and he found himself with little support from media or radio stations. It was a harsh

LEFT Gary at the 1992 Smash Hits Awards, where the group won seven categories

blow.

Maybe cruelly, Robbie made fun of Gary by including the lyrics "Where has Gary Barlow gone?" in a track at the end of his album *Escapology*. It was too much for the vulnerable Gary, who confined himself to the recording studio as a writer and producer. He established himself as president of True North Productions, where to date he has worked with Elton John, Delta Goodrem, Donny Osmond and Christina Aguilera, to name but a few. His own record label, Future Records, was launched in 2009.

He wasn't going to hide away for ever and when the television documentary about Take That was shown to a mass audience it led to the revival of the band. The group reformed, without Robbie, in 2006 and Gary was back where he belonged – leading the phenomenal band on the road to fame and stardom.

Take That didn't just provide Barlow with a successful five-year career combined with fame and fortune; he also met his wife Dawn Andrews through the band, for whom she was a dancer. The couple married in 1999 and they have three children: Daniel, Emily and Daisy. Gary's domestic happiness made Robbie

retract his previous taunting of his former friend, stating that he would swap his fame and success for Gary's family life.

My Take, Barlow's autobiography, was published by Bloomsbury and first issued in hardback. The paperback that followed included an additional chapter that took the reader nearer to the present day with his comeback with the band and the 2007 tour. Until its publication, Gary remained resolutely quiet about himself, despite the huge amount of media interest and articles that were written about him.

In the book, Gary describes the highs and lows he experienced when Take That split in 1996. He enjoyed a promising start to his solo career, but then had a crisis of confidence. His once adoring fans had found other singers to fawn over and the hero worship that had once followed him everywhere was all but gone. The book also reveals how Gary found life on the road with Take That and his truth about the rumours of the infamous feuds that went on.

He starts with his early life, growing up in Cheshire and how his life on the club circuit changed for ever when he met Martin-Smith. The singer also tells

RIGHT Gary with his new wife Dawn, in the West Indies

of the situation when he and Robbie went through a very public falling–out. What does come across from the book is Gary's ever–present determination and positive attitude. This spirit has enabled him to make a graceful and timely comeback.

Meanwhile, despite his own performing career suddenly taking off again with Take That, he has been a successful songwriter for artists such as Charlotte Church, Atomic Kitten, Delta Goodrem, H & Claire, Will Young, Amy Studt, Graham Gouldman and Blue.

It must have been an amazing feeling for Gary when *Forever Love*, his first solo single, made the Number 1 spot in the UK charts. *So Help Me Girl* made the Number 11 slot while *Open Road*, the title track from the album, made it to the Top 10, peaking at Number 7. *Are You Ready Now* also hit the Top 10 at Number 8 and *Hang On In There Baby* – which was the sixth and final single released from the album – climbed to Number 12.

Stronger made it to Number 16 in the UK charts while *For All That You Want* peaked just outside the Top 20

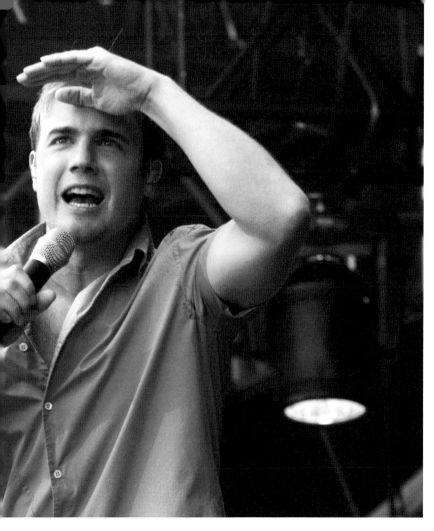

GARY BARLOW

LEFT Gary
fronting the band
in 2007

at Number 24. Of the twelve titles included on *Open Road*, half were self-penned numbers. Two others, *My Commitment* and *Lay Down For Love*, were collaborations with other songwriters and only four songs were written by others, including Madonna. It was followed two years later by a second album, *Twelve Months, Eleven Days*, which peaked at Number 35 in the UK charts.

Gary's next album release came in 2012, when Sing zoomed to the top of the UK charts and gave him a number one single, also titled Sing. Late the following year he released Since I Saw You Last, which went double platinum in the UK and earned Gary a number two single in Let Me Go. By this time his popularity and important contribution to the British music industry had been recognised with the award of an OBE.

Even though Gary all but lost his fans when Robbie made it as a songwriter and performer, he is well and truly back, strong, ready and with his legendary spirit set to continue his huge contribution to the British music scene. He has helped Take That reclaim their place in pop history.

Mark Owen

LEFT Mark at the 1993 Smash Hits Awards

Born in Cheshire on 27 January 1972, Mark Anthony Patrick Owen was educated in Oldham. He worked in retail and a high street bank before he found his true destiny with Take That in 1990. But the music business couldn't have been further removed from his dreams of becoming a professional football player. Mark had trials for Manchester United, Huddersfield Town and Rochdale but suffered a serious injury that put paid to his first-choice career.

He was the third member of Take That to start a solo career, after Gary and Robbie, and his first record, *Child*, reached Number 3 in the UK charts in 1996. It was followed by *Clementine*, which also peaked at Number 3. Mark's 1997 debut album, *Green Man*, left him disappointed when it only climbed to Number 33 in the album charts, and he was dropped by label BMG later the same year when his third single, *I Am What I Am*, only just made it into the Top 30 at Number 29.

For six years, Mark's life turned in a different direction, but he made a personal comeback on Channel Four's *Celebrity Big Brother* in 2002. His win in the second series of the reality show returned him well and truly to the spotlight, and a deal with Island/ Universal Records saw him make it back into the charts in August 2003 with *Four Minute Warning*, his first single in a number of years, peaking at Number 5. The single stayed in the UK Top 40 for eight weeks and he followed it up with a second album, *In Your Own Time*.

Released in November 2003, the album reached Number 39 while the single *Alone Without You* charted at Number 26. But once again, Mark was dropped by his record label and, fed up with being overlooked, he created Sedna Records in April 2004. As well as setting up his own record company, Mark was also busy writing material for his next album, and *How The Mighty Fall* was recorded in Sunset Studios, Los Angeles later that year and released in the UK in 2005.

Produced by Tony Hoffer, *How The Mighty Fall* was launched on April 18 and included the tracks *They Do*, *Sorry Lately*, *Waiting For the Girl*, *3:15*, *Wasting Away*, *Stand* and *Come On*. The three singles that Mark released from the album were *Makin' Out*, which reached Number 30 in the UK charts, *Believe In The Boogie*, which didn't fare well when it reached Number 57, and *Hail Mary*, which was released in December and could not break into the Top 100.

Before his collaboration with Hoffer, who was renowned for his work with the likes of Supergrass, the Thrills and Turin Brakes, Mark worked with the legendary John Leckie, who was responsible for the first solo album, *Green Man*. As one of the UK's most acclaimed producers, Leckie began his career as a tape operator and engineer at Abbey Road Studios. He worked with George Harrison on *All Things Must Pass* and John Lennon's *Plastic Ono Band* as well as Pink Floyd's mega-selling *Dark Side Of The Moon*. He began in production in the mid–1970s but left Abbey Road to become a freelance producer in 1978. Leckie is probably best known for his work with the Stone Roses on their legendary 1989

debut album. As well as working with Mark Owen, he was an important part of the team with the Verve on the album *A Storm In Heaven* and on Radiohead's *The Bends*. Mark had approached Leckie about his album because he wanted to portray an image closer to indie Britpop than Take That had been known for – and Leckie's experience made him the ideal man for the job.

Like Gary Barlow, Jason Orange and Howard Donald, Mark was brought back to the public's attention by the hugely successful television documentary about Take That in 2006. The band's singles *Patience* (released in 2006) and *Shine* (2007) both made it to Number 1 in the UK charts. It was the relaunch that Mark's career needed and Take That's single *I'd Wait For Life* was released in June 2007 prior to the group's huge tour.

Rumours of a further Mark Owen solo album in 2007 proved unfounded, but if fans were disappointed then, they will be content that the 'cute one' in Take That continues to pledge his future to the band.

In his personal life, Owen dated art student Joanna Kelly after leaving Take That and then lived in the Lake District with actress Chloe Bailey. Mark

MARK OWEN

RIGHT Back on stage in 2006 as a member of Take That

and actress Emma Ferguson had a son, Elwood Jack, who was born in August 2006. Despite the birth, the couple decided to cancel their marriage plans the same year. But, in December 2006, the couple announced their plans to marry, and daughter Willow Rose was born in November 2008. Finally, on 8 November 2009, the couple tied the knot at Cawdor Church in Scotland.

But their relationship has had more than its fair share of tricky moments, as Mark revealed to the world in March 2010. That was when the singer said that he had carried on an affair from late 2004 until just before the wedding in October 2009. There had also been ten other affairs, he confessed. Days later, he checked himself into rehab in a bid to deal with issues including heavy drinking.

Mark relaunched his solo career in 2013 when he released his fourth studio album, The Art of Doing Nothing. It proved to be his best-selling solo effort, peaking at number 29 in the UK album chart, and he promoted the release with a tour of the UK and Germany before turning his attention to the forthcoming Take That album, due to be released in late 2014.

Howard Donald

Howard Paul Donald was born on 28 April 1968 at home in Droylsden, Manchester to Kathleen and Keith. As time passed and the family grew, he found himself in the middle with two older brothers, Michael and Colin, a younger brother, Glenn, and a younger sister, Samantha. Perhaps it was this position that lay at the root of him wanting to be a performer, or perhaps it was the fact that it was in his blood: his mother was a singer, his father a Latin American dance teacher.

Attending Moorside primary school and Littlemoss High School for Boys, Howard passed exams in English, Geography and Mathematics, but he was by no means a model pupil, preferring to spend his time breakdancing and riding his BMX bike. His early ambition was to be a pilot, but by the time he had left school he had modified his plans and soon took up an apprenticeship with Manchester car spraying concern Knibbs. Having

completed the apprenticeship, he got his first full-time job working as a spray painter for Wimpole Garages.

Meanwhile, Howard was continuing to improve his breakdancing and had joined a crew called the RDS Royal. Crews tended to congregate at the Manchester Apollo, where one night, Howard was very impressed with the dancing of a member of the rival Street Machine crew. It was Jason Orange. They got talking, discovered they felt the same way about a lot of things and had had many similar experiences, so they decided to leave their crews, pool their resources and form Streetbeat.

Shortly afterwards, Howard and Jason approached Nigel Martin-Smith to see if he would be interested in being their manager. He was impressed but realised that dancing needed to be allied to singing and songwriting to form the perfect pop package. It just so happened that he had a project forming in the back of his mind. Martin-Smith introduced Howard and Jason to Gary and Mark,

who were also on his books. Once Robbie had joined to form the quintet, Take That were up and running.

Although he, Jason and Mark were inevitably confined mostly to backing vocals, chosen for their excellent movement and well-chiselled looks, it was the chemistry of the group that was so crucial. Besides that, Howard did have occasional moments at the centre of the stage, which proved he could more than carry a tune. In fact, Howard took lead vocals on *If This Is Love*, the live version of *Why Can't I Wake Up With You* and, most affectingly, the anthem *Never Forget* that was to prove such a pertinent swansong for the band in its original formation.

After Take That finally split in 1996, Howard was probably the most devastated of all the band members. It didn't help that gremlins jumped all over his plans when he decided to go solo. He recorded a single, *Speak Without Words*, and even got as far as filming a video for it in Cuba before things went wrong at the record company and they decided not to release it. The same neglect was unfortunately foisted upon the album

Howard recorded, about which he reminisces fondly.

As a songwriter, he donated the song *Crazy Chance* to Kavana, another of Martin-Smith's solo acts – it made Number 35 in the charts in May 1996 and, re-released in September 1997, rose to Number 16. He then tried his hand at being a DJ, going out under the name of DJ HD and releasing a single, *Take Control*.

Howard rapidly established an appreciative audience in clubs and student unions, particularly in the North West, by playing a mixture of "uplifting, chunky house and soulful grooves". His fame then spread to Ibiza and to the dance floors of Austria, Germany and Switzerland – and on and on, around the world. In fact, he enjoys this type of performing so much and has been so successful at it that he still continues to DJ to this day, when he's not working with Take That.

Apart from guesting with Gary at a Prince's Trust concert, he hadn't performed live on stage for ten years, but he was interested to answer the call for a reunion, however temporary he thought it might be, although he

HOWARD DONALD

confesses that he has been staggered by the depth of feeling in the response. "I thought most people had moved on with their lives," he says. "I knew there was some interest because we had finished on top, and you still heard the records on the radio, and people sometimes went on about what a good group we were and what a great live act. But I didn't think people would be interested in rushing out and buying these tickets for a live show.

"We didn't have that confidence to

say let's stick in all these twenty dates at once. We just released a few dates to start with but they sold like hot cakes and we had to release the others straight away. We were overwhelmed by it all."

By general consent, Howard's interviews in the TV documentary *Take That – For The Record* which inspired the band to reform were perhaps the wittiest and most trenchant. From comments about the band's notorious first video shoot ("I was cleaning jelly out of my a******* for the next two years") to his self-laceration when he wanted to throw himself in the Thames after the band split ("I wanted to kill myself but I'm just too much of a s******* to do it"), he rivalled the loquacious Robbie for quotability – no mean feat.

As is the way of things, the revived interest in Take That has stimulated greater interest in Howard's work as a DJ, so he is now probably busier than ever. His solution to marrying his twin careers is to arrange that he performs as a DJ around dates wherever the group plays. He parties on.

Howard is the father of two young daughters, Grace and Lola.

Jason Orange

Jason was born in Manchester on 10 July 1970, along with his twin brother, Justin, to Jenny and Tony. He was one of a large family: as well as his other brothers Simon, Dominic, Samuel and Oliver, he also has two half-sisters, Emma and Amy, a stepbrother, also called Simon, and a stepsister, Sarah.

By his own admission, Jason's schooldays were not exactly overflowing with achievement. He attended primary school at Haveley Hey in Wythenshawe, before going on to South Manchester High School. There he gained most enjoyment from non-academic subjects, with a particular liking for sports such as football, swimming and athletics. So he left school at sixteen with few qualifications and even fewer regrets.

At first, he and Justin joined a local Youth Training Scheme, and he ended up employed as a painter and decorator for an organisation called Direct Works. Jason found this an acceptable way to earn a crust, but he soon decided he didn't want to do it for the rest of his life.

He was really into breakdancing and joined a crew called Street Machine, with whom he was soon demonstrating his talents. He got noticed, and it was not long before he was invited to appear on a TV programme, called *The Hit Man And Her*, with Pete Waterman and Michaela Strachan.

Around this time, he met Howard Donald, who was in a rival breakdancing crew. They got on so well that they decided to quit their respective crews and form a new breakdancing duo, Streetbeat. Soon afterwards, they approached Nigel Martin-Smith and the rest is history.

Although it sometimes seemed that, along with Howard and Mark, Jason was merely in Take That to provide good-looking back-up to Gary and Robbie, the true situation was far more complex than that. As subsequent events showed, the chemistry between the band members was of great importance. However, his singing was often the butt of jokes from Gary, who once, in

response to Jason's request to write a song for him, said he already had done – but it was an instrumental.

Jason was hit quite hard by the break-up of Take That, and his entirely natural response was to take a long holiday from show business. He went backpacking around the world for a year or two, during which time he learned to mellow out and live a simple life at hostels. The only exceptions where when he was recognised and was forced to check into five-star hotels to escape the unwanted attentions of eager groupies. During his travels, he particularly enjoyed visiting Thailand, Malaysia and New Zealand, keeping a diary of his thoughts before returning home and moving on to New York to enrol in an acting course.

When he finally returned once more to England, Jason found work in television, playing the part of Brent Moyer, an insidious drug-dealing DJ, in the 1999 production of Lynda La Plante's *Killer Net*. He also featured in two plays, firstly in *Let's All Go To The Fair* at the Royal Court Theatre, London, and, more prominently, as a haranguing street-poet in *Gob* by James

Kenworth, directed by James Martin Charlton at the King's Head Theatre, also in London.

By all accounts, Jason turned in professional performances, but he felt he just wasn't cut out to be an actor. Perceptively, he noticed that he always felt as though he was acting, whereas true actors would be actually living the part. It was a boundary that he was going to find difficult to cross. The transition from performing live in front of 20,000 fans to acting for a handful of theatregoers was also hard. So he drifted away from television and the theatre.

This time, Jason decided to fill the gaps in his education. He enrolled in a course at South Trafford College studying psychology and sociology, two subjects that had increasingly fascinated him during his time in the band and thereafter. Although he had now deliberately slipped out of the public eye, he wasn't completely dormant because he still attended charity gigs and functions.

However, when the call came for the group members to work together on the tenth anniversary TV programme, *Take That – For The Record*, he decided he was ready to return to the

LEFT
Howard and Jason sharing a microphone on tour in 2006

JASON ORANGE

RIGHT More
at home singing,
rather than acting

BELOW
Jason in 2001

fray, however briefly. And when the enthusiastic response to the broadcast and the simultaneously released *The Ultimate Collection – Never Forget* meant that a tour was in the offing, he was ready for that as well. But he was very aware that the group would have to take infinite pains if they were going to try to interest the public in an album of fresh songs. With disarming candour,

he points out: "You can sell a tour on nostalgia, and we did. But you can't sell new material based on nostalgia – it's got to be quality."

It was. The album, *Beautiful World*, more than lived up to expectations. And Jason even got to sing his first lead vocal on the song *Wooden Boat*. Fair enough; he wrote it. Lead vocals on other songs have followed.

He has a more thoughtful, considered approach to life and music fifteen years on, as can be gauged by his involvement in the songwriting labours. It is far less likely, for instance, that he would be unable to remember whether or not he enjoyed the sexual favours of a certain female star.

On the pressures of diving back into the goldfish bowl of superstardom, Jason was more interested in noting his family's reactions. "One or two of them had reservations but the rest were very keen," he said at the time. "The first time around my youngest brother was in school and I didn't consider that at the time. It was a real pain for him to have a famous older brother but he's twenty-six now and it's cool."

Robbie's Departure & The Break-up

It often does not take much for youngsters who have enjoyed incredible success and earned unbelievable sums of money to go off the rails, and that was what seemed to be happening to Robbie Williams in the final twelve months of his Take That career.

Robbie was struggling to control drink and drug habits that were becoming an embarrassment to the other members of the group. At the Glastonbury Festival in 1995 he was clearly out of control, falling out of a Rolls Royce clutching bottles of champagne and partying with the bad boy of rock, Liam Gallagher of Oasis. Pictures of Robbie were plastered across the newspapers, as were quotes he had been dishing out in unofficial interviews, but he claims to have no memories of the weekend whatsoever.

Rumours soon began to circulate that Robbie was going to leave the group, and these were confirmed on July 17. The official statement read that Robbie "was no longer able to give Take That the commitment they needed" and refunds were offered to fans who had bought tickets for the forthcoming tour with the intention of seeing him.

"The Glastonbury thing was a problem," Mark Owen explained later. "It wasn't why Rob left the band but it did start the break-up. We'd worked for five years and had looked after what was going on around us – we built a wall around us for five years. You become protective and if people want to do an interview with you they have to go through the proper channels, so what happened at Glastonbury did p★★s us off …"

ROBBIE'S DEPARTURE & THE BREAK-UP

RIGHT
Now a foursome,
Take That on
stage in 1995

It emerged that tension had been
building between Robbie and Gary
Barlow, something those in the know
had seen looming on the horizon, as
A&R man Nick Raymonde explained:
"It was always going to be Gary and
Robbie that clashed and you could
see that was ultimately going to end
in tears."

But it also became apparent that
Robbie's partying was not received well
by the other members of the group and
his four band-mates allegedly cornered
him one night in rehearsal and said
that they were thinking about doing
the next tour as a four-piece and asked
him for his opinion. Needless to say,
Robbie knew he wasn't wanted and
departed, though he did later admit that
he cried because it was over. But he also
explained that he had had enough of
people's egos and mind games.

Having already completed the
recording of their third album *Nobody
Else*, the band could hardly delete
Robbie's contribution, and the first
single, *Never Forget*, was released very
soon after the split. It became their
seventh Number 1 but there wouldn't
have been many punters who would

ROBBIE'S DEPARTURE & THE BREAK-UP

RIGHT It's official... Take That wave goodbye at a press conference in 1996

have risked their hard-earned cash with a bet that this would be Take That's last release before their farewell offering seven months later. As 1996 began, the press began publishing stories that the remaining four members were not going to continue, and this was confirmed on February 13.

It was announced that their cover of the Bee Gees' *How Deep Is Your Love*, taken from the forthcoming *Greatest Hits* compilation, would be their last single. Such was the depth of feeling felt by fans across the globe that helplines were set up to help them deal with their devastation.

It was never publicly acknowledged that the reason for the band's demise was Robbie's departure, but Mark did later admit that it was never the same once they had slimmed down to a foursome.

Gary and Mark announced their intentions to concentrate on their solo careers and nobody categorically stated that the band would never reform. They appeared at the Brit Awards and played their supposed final gig in Amsterdam on 5 April 1996.

While Gary was initially quite philosophical about his former band-mate's potential solo success, a verbal war soon gripped the public's attention. He had admitted prior to the release of *Forever Love* that "Robbie is ten times more popular than I am. There is no contest. His record is out three weeks after mine. Well, if I'm Number 1 for three weeks, I'll be pleased."

Robbie, meanwhile, was soon engaging in derogatory comments such as: "I hate you, Barlow. Gary's selfish, greedy, arrogant and thick. He's a clueless w★★★★★". But he was not totally putting down the songwriter as he did admit: "To be honest, I know Gary can do better. I know he's got brilliant songs and I know that his album's title track, *Open Road*, is a fantastic song. It's another *Back For Good*, and that was the best song Take That ever did … Gary should have a brilliant solo career. He's a very good songwriter."

It seemed it would take time to heal the rift between Robbie and the other members of Take That, but Robbie was noticeably absent when Gary, Mark, Jason and Howard did reform, although they had clearly left the door open for him. History shows that he eventually pushed at that door.

For The Record: The TV Documentary

RIGHT Take That at the preview screening of their TV documentary

" "You know, our dream is that after five or ten years, we'll come back and do it all over again." When Gary uttered these words at the press conference in Manchester on 13 February 1996 to announce that the band were breaking up, he probably had little idea how prescient his thoughts were.

OK, so five years passed by without a peep, but he was dead right on the second count. Towards the end of 2004, the possibility of relaunching a greatest hits package was mooted and found favour.

So when the idea was first broached to broadcast a TV documentary to mark the tenth anniversary of the break-up of the band, the members were interested but wary. Would it just be an endless series of boring talking heads saying how they loved the band or, alternatively, couldn't stand them? Or maybe just a mindless collection of vaguely amusing stories strung together about young girls getting overexcited at concerts? Gary, Howard, Jason and Mark decided it wasn't going to be that way.

On the contrary, they agreed, the programme would feature their own recollections of what happened. And, crucially, Robbie declared himself interested. This guaranteed, if guarantee were needed, that there would be no lack of candour in the making of the programme.

Meanwhile, a repackaged greatest hits collection would be released in the same week. These simultaneous actions would demonstrate whether Take That were still of any relevance to the outside world. It proved to be a

RIGHT Back
in the limelight,
Take That pose
for the cameras

marketing masterstroke.

Seven million people watched the broadcast on 16 November 2005. In these days of fragmented TV audiences, this figure far exceeded expectations for a band that had been out of the public eye for such a long time. The story was the key – it was a gripping one. Threading its way through the personalities and the music, it was a classic showbiz tale of rise and fall.

The documentary told the story of the band from the very early days trekking around the country in Nigel Martin-Smith's beaten-up car. It covered those first concerts and the early videos, before moving on to take in all the trappings of burgeoning success. The cameras took in the pounding excitement of the arena concerts, the almost maniacal reactions of their fans, the security guards fearful for the group's lives (and their own), illuminated in a few short interviews with some of those fans and guards involved.

Mark remembers what the madness was like at its height: "We were heading towards a hotel in Italy. It was off the beaten track but the road at either side was packed with people

RIGHT Back in the limelight, Take That pose for the cameras

ABOVE
There has never
been a lack of
fans for Take That

all chasing the bus. There was a lot of mayhem going on, people were just running down the streets screaming and shouting as we arrived at this hotel with the police escorts. That,

for me, summed up what it was like being in that band, with all the travelling around the world, and all the craziness."

The documentary also took in

the inevitable decline. It showed the beginnings of the rebellion against managerial rule, some of the intra-band rivalry, Robbie's drink and drug binges, his departure from the band, the tight-lipped conviction that "the show must go on", the final tour, the even more final break-up. There was also footage of four of the band (Robbie didn't make it) meeting up in a hotel to discuss old times, like members of a successful football team or veteran soldiers.

Despite not turning up for the reunion, Robbie was still able to provide good copy. On Nigel Martin-Smith: "He's definitely in the top three most disturbed individuals I've ever worked with. I only ever wanted him to love me. That's the really sad thing. And he never did." The former Svengali metaphorically shakes his head. On wanting to leave the group, Robbie explains he had his head up his own backside at the time. He tells Howard, Jason and Mark what good guys they are. He apologises for calling Gary a crap songwriter. At the reunion, the other four mumble about what a hard time he had of it.

ABOVE 'The Ultimate Tour' was a sell-out

What set the programme apart was the excellent backstage footage, where little seemed to have been censored and the banter sizzled to and fro. Take That had dared to offer the audience a full measure of honesty and realism, and they were duly rewarded for taking what is often seen as a sizeable risk.

Not only was it a highly rated critical success, it also registered very strongly with the fans. It's quite possible that maybe they saw another side to the band, and liked what they saw.

The other side of the marketing equation had proceeded according to plan. *The Ultimate Collection – Never Forget* had been released in the same week as the TV show and rose rapidly to Number 2 in the album charts. The band were back in the news.

Nominated for an award in the Arts and Specials Category of the Rose d'Or (the Golden Rose) held in Lucerne in April 2006, the documentary's life continued. When the DVD was released in the same month, with obligatory extra footage, it sold exceptionally well.

Also in that same month, the group began 'The Ultimate Tour' (which has happily proved to be a misnomer, since it has turned out not to be their last) – an arenas and stadiums tour of the British Isles, which included six shows at Wembley Arena and at Birmingham NEC, three at Manchester MEN Arena, two each at Dublin's The Point, Glasgow SECC, Newcastle Metro and Sheffield Hallam Arena, and a visit to the Odyssey Arena in Belfast.

The stadium shows comprised two each at the Milton Keynes National Bowl and the City of Manchester Stadium, as well as trips to the Millennium Stadium in Cardiff and the RDS Stadium in Dublin.

The hysteria, albeit a little more controlled this time around, was happening all over again.

LEFT The boys backstage at Wembley Arena, 2006

Greatest Hits

RIGHT Signing copies of their latest album *Beautiful World*

These days, it seems anyone can put together a greatest hits compilation even if they've only released a couple of albums. In the early days of such projects, bands often had to wait nearly ten years before their record company would consider such a proposal. Indeed, Queen issued eight albums before their first *Greatest Hits* was released in 1981.

Of course, if a band decides to call it a day then their record company will quickly cash in on their popularity before it fades, and this was the case with Take That. Not that the group's popularity has faded at all in the intervening years, as their reformation has proved. Just three months after the announcement that shocked their fans, RCA Records released a compilation of Take That's hits that stormed to the top of the UK charts.

Greatest Hits

Highest UK chart position:
Number 1
Year: 1996
Containing all of Take That's single

successes – including the US version of *Love Ain't Here Anymore* – *Greatest Hits* has sold more than a million copies in the UK alone.

Never Forget – The Ultimate Collection

Highest UK chart position:
Number 2
Year: 2005
This was basically the same as the previous compilation but also included a live version of *Pray* and a remix of *Relight My Fire*. It was also notable for the inclusion of a new track, *Today I've Lost You*. This was originally written as the follow-up to *Back For Good* but was never released after the group disbanded. The track was recorded in September 2005 and was then performed on the Ultimate Tour with Gary's wife, Dawn, dancing on stage.

The album – which has also sold more than two million copies in the UK – reached Number 2 in the chart

RIGHT
Take That
savouring
the thrill of
performing 'live'
again

and was accompanied by a DVD featuring videos of the songs.

The Platinum Collection

Highest UK chart position: Number 127
Year: 2006

November 2006 saw the re-release of *Take That And Party*, *Everything Changes* and *Nobody Else* with bonus tracks to coincide with the group's return. These three albums were also combined in a three-disc box-set, *The Platinum Collection*, which offered fans who already owned the CDs the chance to buy something a little bit different.

Three tracks were added to the band's debut offering – *Waiting Around*, *How Can It Be* and *Guess Who Tasted Love* (Edit) – while the band's 1993 release was extended by four tracks (*No, Si Aqui No Hay Amor*, *The Party Remix*, *All I Want Is You* and *Babe* (Return Mix)). The bonus tracks on the third disc were two remixes of *Sure* and *Back For Good*, along with a live version of *Every Guy*.

LITTLE BOOK OF **TAKE THAT**   95

Beautiful World
Tour 2007

And so the wheels of the mighty circus began to turn in earnest once more. Towards the end of February 2007, the band announced they would be undertaking a major European and UK tour near the end of the year. They would hone their Beautiful World stage show to perfection on a tour of Australia, Canada and Japan during the summer.

As a taster for the tour, the group appeared at the Concert for Diana on 1 July 2007 at Wembley Stadium to mark the ten years that had passed since the Princess of Wales had died in Paris. The concert was held on what would have been her forty-sixth birthday. Members of the group rescheduled time off to fit in the show, because, according to Mark: "Diana was an inspiration to so many people and we feel privileged to have met her." The group once took

tea with her at Kensington Palace, which Mark cites as a highlight of their career. "We decided we wanted to do anything we [could] to make Diana's concert one of the highlights of the summer."

Predictably, for the second European tour of the reunited Take That, every date of the fifty was completely sold out, with all tickets being snapped up within forty minutes of going on sale.

For every show except one, Sophie Ellis-Bextor performed as the group's special guest. The final show of the tour – on the final day of 2007 – at London's O2 Arena on 31 December 2007 was billed as Countdown to Midnight: Take That & Sugababes. The glamorous girl group performed for twenty-five minutes before Take That took to the stage at 11.50 pm and carried the ecstatic crowd with them into 2008.

BEAUTIFUL WORLD TOUR 2007

That O2 gig was the final night of a
tour that found favour with critics and
fans alike. Altogether, the band played
the O2 nine times, with audiences
totalling 132,835 and box office money
exceeding $10 million. The 'Take
That at Midnight' setlist that saw in
the new year kicked off with *Shine*
and *Patience* before a rocking version
of the traditional *Auld Lang Syne* and
an almost-traditional *Relight My Fire*.
The set continued with *Rule the World*
and *Could it be Magic* before the crowd
joined in with a sing-along medley. The
show then reached a climax with *Back
for Good* and *Never Forget*.

Naturally, that set differed from the
normal offering that the band played in
European venues from Belfast to Milan.
It kicked off with *Reach Out* and *It Only
Takes a Minute* before continuing with
Beautiful World, *Patience*, *Hold On* and
I'd Wait for Life. The show carried on
with *Relight my Fire*, *Rule the World* and
Could it be Magic before audiences got
their chance to shine with the sing-
along medley. Next up were *Back for
Good*, *Everything Changes*, *Wooden Boat*
and *Give Good Feeling*, before the band
continued with *Sure*, *Never Forget*, *Shine*

and *Pray*. It was then time for the outro and the band's farewells.

Besides the London dates, the tour encompassed five shows in Belfast and Birmingham, an extraordinary eleven in Manchester's MEN Arena – a happy homecoming – three in Glasgow and two in Newcastle upon Tyne. Germany got six shows and Denmark and Italy two each, while Spain, Austria, Switzerland and the Netherlands also got in on the act.

As we have seen, the tour was a massive success, but it wasn't all plain sailing. As the DVD that resulted from the tour showed, during the gig in Vienna's Stadthalle on October 26, Howard Donald came to grief during a jump in *Sure* and "felt a crack". In hospital, it was discovered that he had suffered a collapsed lung, and he was out of action until November 7, when the band played in Oberhausen, Germany. Meanwhile, the band continued as a three-piece, with Howard making fleeting appearances to greet the crowd at the beginning of shows. On one occasion, he turned up on stage wearing a hospital gown which showed a cheeky expanse of backside when he turned round. Another time, he delighted the crowd by appearing in drag.

The tour was, of course, a phenomenal showcase for the *Beautiful World* album, which had been released on 24 November 2006 and was the group's first album offering for eleven years. Certified gold in Italy and Switzerland, the album has reached platinum status in Germany, twice platinum in Ireland and – wait for it – eight times platinum status in the UK. It has sold well over three million copies worldwide and, in the UK, was the second best-selling album of 2006 despite only being on sale for one month. It followed up by becoming the fourth best-selling album of 2007 and the thirty-third best-selling of 2008. Needless to say, its peak position in the UK and Ireland album charts was Number 1.

Beautiful World marked a departure for Take That in that every member of the band – except for Robbie, of course, but that would come – took lead vocals on at least one song. The BBC's Julie Broadfoot was more than happy with the album, and said it had a "more mature sound. It's pop but without the cheese … Their voices are stronger and the lead vocals (and writing credits) are shared … It's a heart-warming album that fans will love."

And love it the fans certainly did, just as they loved the sight of Take That on the stages of the world.

LEFT
London's
O2 Arena –
still under
construction
in 2007

Never Forget – The Stage Musical

RIGHT
Hopefuls queue
during the first
day of open
auditions for the
musical *Never
Forget*

You know when you've made a lasting impression on the world when your songs are turned into a musical. The likes of Queen (*We Will Rock You*), ABBA (*Mamma Mia!*), Rod Stewart (*Tonight's The Night*) and Buddy Holly (*Buddy The Musical*) have been honoured in this fashion and 2007 saw Take That join this elite group when *Never Forget – The Take That Musical* received its premiere at the Wales Millennium Centre in Cardiff on July 20.

Although it was originally the idea of the band's choreographer, Kim Gavin, it was Danny Brocklehurst – creator of hit shows such as *Shameless* and *Clocking Off* – who was responsible for writing the musical with Guy Jones and Ed Curtis.

Based around a fictional Take That tribute band and set in Manchester – where else? – the show followed hero Ash through highs and lows with his best friends in a comedy of love, friendship, ambition and betrayal. It was not intended to be a biographical story but it was packed full of Take That hits from the 1990s including *Pray*, *Relight My Fire*, *Babe*, *Back For Good* and, of course, *Never Forget*.

It was directed by Ed Curtis (*Conspiracy* and *Marlon Brando's Corset*), choreographed by Karen Bruce (*Footloose* and *Fame*) and co-produced by Tristan Baker, whose credits include *Kiss Me Kate*, *Little Shop Of Horrors* and *Calamity Jane*.

After its stint in Cardiff, the musical went on tours of the UK before opening in London's Savoy Theatre on 7 May 2008. Having gained mostly favourable reviews, it closed after a six-month run.

NEVER FORGET - THE STAGE MUSICAL

"We are creating a spectacle which will appeal to both Take That fans and musical theatregoers alike," said co-producer Bronia Buchanan at the time. "We hope that the band will be delighted with the production when they see the show themselves."

But stories had surfaced in April 2007 that legal action was being considered to prevent the musical from going into production. Gary Barlow, in particular, was damning about the project at the time, claiming: "I'm furious and I'll do everything legally possible to stop the show, which has the smell of the end of a pier about it."

"We are the biggest fans of Take That's music," Baker countered, "and we are so excited about the wonderful opportunity to create a new musical based on the fantastic catalogue of their work. We look forward to creating a legacy with these well-loved songs in the way that shows such as *Mamma Mia!* have done before."

In the end, the band distanced themselves from the production with a statement that read: "[The band] would wish their fans and the general

public to know that this production is absolutely and 100 per cent nothing to do with Take That."

Even Gary was won round in the end, though. After the musical's London opening, he admitted: "The reports I've seen have been really good, so there must be something good in it. I'm just worried that they're better than us."

And Robbie
Makes Five

The rumours of a return to Take That for Robbie Williams were, as ever, circulating as the band released their fifth studio album, *The Circus*, in December 2008. The fact that the full reunion was still some way off did nothing to deter fans rushing out to the record stores on the day of release – in fact, many thousands couldn't even wait that long.

Already given a taster of the album in the shape of the *Greatest Day* single, released in November, fans got their preorders for the album in early. By the time of its launch, it had become the most preordered album in pop music history, and the sales didn't stop there. First week sales were 432,490, the third highest of all time in the UK. Needless to say, *The Circus* hit Number 1 in the charts, and it stayed there for five weeks. It would be March 2010 before

it dropped out of the charts altogether.

But it wasn't that long before plans for a stadium tour to promote the album were announced – and more records were broken as tickets sold at an extraordinary rate. In the end, the tour was seen by more than a million people in the UK and Ireland, but the original eight concerts were sold out in less than five hours.

The tour started on 5 June 2009 with two dates in Sunderland's Stadium of Light before going on to visit the Ricoh Arena, Coventry (three concerts), Dublin's Croke Park, the Millennium Stadium in Cardiff (two dates), Hampden Park in Glasgow (three dates), Manchester's Old Trafford cricket ground (no fewer than five concerts) and Wembley Stadium. Here, the band, with special guests James Morrison, the Script

AND ROBBIE MAKES FIVE

RIGHT
Robbie had been
writing with Gary
unknown to fans

and Lady Gaga, played four concerts, bringing the tour to a close on July 5. It took just a few months after the end of the tour for a live album, with a bonus disc recorded in the Abbey Road studios, to be released, and fans not satisfied with that could also buy DVDs or Blu-rays of two of the Wembley concerts. And many fans did just that, with the DVD becoming the fastest-selling of all time in the UK on its day of release.

Meanwhile, the singles from *The Circus* – first *Up All Night*, then *Said It All* and *Hold Up a Light* – kept coming, and kept making the charts. The album had been well received by critics as well as fans, with the BBC saying it was a "stunning album ... Take That are the vintage champagne of pop fizzing with playful bubbles and happily maturing with age."

But what so many fans had dreamed and talked of for years – the return of Robbie – was closer than many imagined. In the summer of 2010, it emerged that Robbie and Gary had been writing and recording together – something that would have been unthinkable a few short years before.

The result was a single, *Shame*, attributed to Robbie and Gary and featuring both singers on vocals: the first time that had happened since 1995. On release in October, the Trevor Horn-produced record predictably stormed the charts, reaching Number 2 in the UK and performing well all over Europe.

How had this happened? Gary revealed that he and Robbie had started working together in February 2010 in Los Angeles, apparently determined to move on from the feud that had separated the pair for the previous fifteen years. *Shame* had, said Gary, taken less than an hour to write.

But even more incredible events preceded the release of *Shame*. Finally, the rumours were substantiated as, on July 15, a statement released on behalf of Take That and Robbie declared: "Following months of speculation, Gary Barlow, Howard Donald, Jason Orange, Mark Owen and Robbie Williams confirmed they have been recording a new studio album as a five-piece, which they will release in November."

It emerged that work on the album, *Progress*, had started as early as

September 2009, shortly after the end of the Circus tour. All five members of the band had met to begin writing the six songs that would form the foundation of the album.

That their work had not been wasted was confirmed by the enormous number of preorders, which was so high that the album's release had to be brought forward a week, to November 15. The album was preceded a week earlier by the release of a single, *The Flood*, which peaked at Number 2. The album fared better, making the Number 1 spot in its first week and going on to sell well over two million copies in the UK by the spring of 2011. *Progress* had helped Take That become the best-selling artists of all time for the Amazon music store, it was announced.

It was also popular with the critics, and *The Guardian* was especially laudatory in its review, saying: "Take That's first album as a quintet since 1995 is informed by two things: a genuinely new sound and Robbie Williams's seamless reimmersion into life as a band member, which is played out on emotional duets with Gary Barlow and Mark Owen."

LEFT
Robbie had a "seamless reimmersion" into the band

AND ROBBIE MAKES FIVE

RIGHT
Is he back for
good?

So it seemed it was pretty much business as normal for the five-man Take That. It was almost as if the years since 1995 had dissolved, although memories of that feud-driven separation will remain with fans for ever. But in another move that will help to roll back the years, the Progress tour of huge venues in the summer of 2011 proved enormously popular.

Starting, again, at the Stadium of Light in Sunderland on May 27, the tour put its Circus predecessor – and even the likes of Michael Jackson's planned This Is It concerts – in the shade. A record-breaking eight nights at Wembley Stadium followed concerts in Manchester, Cardiff, Dublin, Glasgow and Birmingham, and the tour then moved on to European stages: Milan, Copenhagen, Amsterdam, Hamburg, Düsseldorf and Munich. The final date, in Munich's majestic Olympic Stadium, was July 29.

Faithful Take That fans hoped the Progress tour signalled that the band were back for good. And their hopes rose in late 2013 when news broke of a new album, to be released at Christmas 2014.

The Singles

When *Everything Changes* made its UK chart debut at Number 1 in 1994, it gave Take That the distinction of being the first act since the Beatles, almost thirty years earlier, to register four consecutive chart-toppers. By the time their farewell offering – *How Deep Is Your Love* – entered at the top of the chart two years later, they had become the first artists to see their singles hit the peak of the chart in the first week of release.

Do What U Like
Highest UK chart position: 82
Year: 1991

Co-written by Ray Hedges and Gary Barlow – who also contributed the lead vocals – *Do What You Like* was the group's debut release, but it flopped. Nigel Martin-Smith had selected this track from *Take That And Party*, but sales were hindered by a cheesy video that saw half-naked band members rolling around in jelly. It was later voted the second worst video of all time by VH1.

Promises
Highest UK chart position: 38
Year: 1991

Again written by the Hedges-Barlow partnership, *Promises* proved to be the first Take That single to hit the Top 40. The band members jumped on Robbie's hotel bed so much once they heard the news that it broke.

Once You've Tasted Love
Highest UK chart position: 47
Year: 1992

The band's third offering from their debut album failed to improve on the success of its predecessor. With Gary on lead vocals and Robbie rapping in an attempted American accent, this proved to be the last single for some time to fail to make the Top 15.

It Only Takes A Minute
Highest UK chart position: 7
Year: 1992

Despite Gary's reluctance to release a cover, Take That's rendition of Tavares'

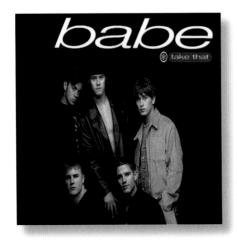

US Number 1 hit from 1975, the disco beat of *It Only Takes A Minute* – with the video featuring the dancing skills of Howard and Jason in particular – found a willing audience in 1992 and saw the band register their first Top 10 entry.

I Found Heaven
Highest UK chart position:15
Year: 1992

The first Take That single on which Robbie got to perform the lead vocals was also the first release not penned by Gary. It was, in fact, written by producers Ian Levine and Billy Griffin, and set the stage for the release of the band's debut album.

A Million Love Songs
Highest UK chart position: 7
Year: 1992

Recorded in just one take, *A Million Love Songs* had been written by Gary many years earlier and established his reputation as one of the best songwriters in Britain in the early 1990s.

Could It Be Magic
Highest UK chart position: 3
Year: 1992

Another cover version was the final release from the boys' debut album and this time it was a Barry Manilow classic from 1975. *Could It Be Magic* saw Take That register their highest chart position to date and it won Best British Single at the Brit Awards.

Why Can't I Wake Up With You
Highest UK chart position: 2
Year: 1993

One of three songs written by Gary at the age of sixteen, *Why Can't I Wake Up With You* was only kept off the top of the chart by 2 Unlimited's dance hit *No Limit*.

Pray
Highest UK chart position: 1
Year: 1993

It was another Barlow composition that gave Take That their first UK chart-topper. *Pray* hit Number 1 in July 1993 and was the first release from their second studio offering, *Everything Changes*.

Relight My Fire
Highest UK chart position: 1
Year: 1993

A collaboration with Lulu saw a second consecutive Number 1 single for Take That and a first for the 1960s songstress.

RIGHT
Take That,
backstage at the
Royal Variety
Performance in
2006

The original plan had been for Robbie to partner Lulu on lead vocals on the Dan Hartman composition, but this was ditched as Gary's voice combined perfectly with the Scot's.

Babe
Highest UK chart position: 1
Year: 1993
With lead vocals from Mark, *Babe* was the answer to everyone's prayers when it knocked Mr Blobby off the top of the chart. Unfortunately for everyone over the age of six, Noel Edmonds' annoying pink creation exacted revenge and claimed the Christmas Number 1 spot the following week.

Everything Changes
Highest UK chart position: 1
Year: 1994
The fifth single from the album of the same name again saw the group at the summit of the charts, where they remained for two weeks. Take That were by now the biggest act in the UK.

Love Ain't Here Anymore
Highest UK chart position: 3
Year: 1994

This was Take That's only single in a three-year period (1993-96) that failed to hit Number 1. Not surprising, really, when you consider that Wet Wet Wet's *Love Is All Around* – the theme from the hit movie *Four Weddings And A Funeral* – was enjoying a four-month stay at the top of the charts.

Sure
Highest UK chart position: 1
Year: 1994
With lead vocals from Gary, Robbie and Mark, *Sure* was the first offering from Take That's third studio album,

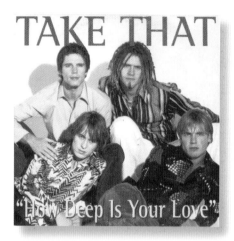

Nobody Else. It also returned the boys to the top of the chart after the hiccup of *Love Ain't Here Anymore*.

Back For Good
Highest UK chart position: 1
Year: 1995
Such was the demand for this single that its release date was advanced by six weeks. Written in just fifteen minutes by Gary, it sold 300,000 copies in its first week and became the band's first US Top 10 hit.

Never Forget
Highest UK chart position: 1
Year: 1995
This was the final Take That single to feature the vocal talents of Robbie, who had left the band just a couple of weeks before its release. It featured home videos of the band members as children and was produced by the legendary Jim Steinman.

How Deep Is Your Love
Highest UK chart position: 1
Year: 1996
The quartet's farewell single was a cover of the Bee Gees' 1977 Number 3 hit. It performed better than the original,

however, giving Take That their eighth UK chart-topper and going on to sell more than 500,000 copies.

Patience
Highest UK chart position: 1
Year: 2006
A return to form after a ten-year hiatus, *Patience* is credited to all four band members plus producer John Shanks. It went on to become the eighth best-selling single of the year and won the boys another Brit Award for Best British Single.

Shine
Highest UK chart position: 1
Year: 2007
The second single to be released from their comeback album *Beautiful World*, *Shine* – featuring Mark on lead vocals – matched the chart success of its predecessor to become Take That's tenth Number 1 hit.

I'd Wait For Life
Highest UK chart position: 17
Year: 2007
With Gary returning to the lead vocal role, *I'd Wait For Life* was the first Take That single to miss out on the Top 10

since 1992 and brought to an end to their run of six Number 1 hits.

Rule the World
Highest UK chart position: 2
Year: 2007

Written by the band for Matthew Vaughn's fantasy movie *Stardust*, *Rule the World* was the fifth single taken from *Beautiful World* and featured lead vocals from Gary and Howard. Only Leona Lewis's *Bleeding Love* prevented it from claiming top spot.

Greatest Day
Highest UK chart position: 1
Year: 2008

The first single taken from *The Circus* album went straight to the top of the charts to become Take That's eleventh Number 1 single. It lasted only one week at the top, however, before being ousted by – you guessed it – Leona Lewis.

Up All Night
Highest UK chart position: 14
Year: 2009

Written by Gary, Howard, Mark, Ben Mark and Jamie Norton, *Up All Night* became the band's twentieth single on the run to make the UK Top 20. It also featured in the last ever episode of the hit TV sitcom *Gavin and Stacey*.

The Garden
Highest UK chart position: 97
Year: 2009

They loved this band-written song in Denmark, where it peaked at Number 8 in the charts. Elsewhere, however, the fans were less enthusiastic. The video was shot at Greenwich Maritime Museum in south east London.

Said it All
Highest UK chart position: 9
Year: 2009

A return to Top 10 form, *Said it All* featured Gary and Mark on lead vocals.

Again taken from *The Circus*, it was written by the band with Steve Robson and became Take That's eighteenth single to break into the Top 10.

The Flood
Highest UK chart position: 2
Year: 2010

Robbie's back! He and Gary shared lead vocals on the only single released in 2010, taken from the *Progress* album. The video featured the five band members taking part in a rowing race past London landmarks and out to sea.

Kidz
Highest UK chart position: 28
Year: 2011

Nick Levine of *Digital Spy* was enthusiastic about the band's first single of 2011. It was a "rabble-rousing glam-disco-pop stomper with ambiguously apocalyptic lyrics and – not inappropriately – one hell of a chorus," he wrote.

Happy Now
Highest UK chart position: 52
Year: 2011

The third single from *Progress* helped to promote the band's Comic Relief appearance.

Love Love
Highest UK chart position: 15
Year: 2011

Taken from the band's *Progressed* EP, Love Love was the official single of the *X-Men: First Class* film.

When We Were Young
Highest UK chart position: 88
Year: 2011

Another movie-linked release, this featured in the new adaptation of *The Three Musketeers*.

LEFT Take That receiving their Brit Award for their single *Patience*, 2007

The Albums

D espite the fact that Take That released just three albums between their arrival on the scene in 1991 and their split five years later, their sales figures stand at an incredible nine million copies worldwide. When their comeback offering, *Beautiful World*, was released in 2006 to rave reviews and huge success, it merely confirmed what their fans have always recognised: Take That are quite simply one of the biggest acts the UK has produced in the last twenty years.

Take That And Party

Highest UK chart position: 2
Year: 1992
Track listing/writer(s):
I Found Heaven
(Billy Griffin/Ian Levine)
Once You've Tasted Love (Gary Barlow)
It Only Takes a Minute (Brian Potter/
Dennis Lambert)
A Million Love Songs (Gary Barlow)
Satisfied (Gary Barlow)
I Can Make It (Gary Barlow)
Do What U Like
(Gary Barlow/Ray Hedges)
Promises (Gary Barlow/Graham Stack)
Why Can't I Why Wake Up with You?
(Gary Barlow)
Never Want to Let You Go
(Gary Barlow)

LEFT
Take That at the
2006 Q Awards

Give Good Feeling (Gary Barlow)
Could it Be Magic (Radio Rappino Mix) (Barry Manilow)
Take That and Party (Gary Barlow, Ray Hedges)
Producer: Duncan Bridgeman
Released on CD in August 1992, Take That And Party debuted in the UK charts at Number 5 before peaking at Number 2, despite competition from Mike Oldfield's *Tubular Bells II* and greatest hits compilations from Kylie Minogue and ABBA. The album spent a staggering seventy-three weeks in the charts and went on to sell more than 750,000 in its first twelve months. It succeeded all expectations as Nigel Martin-Smith had claimed that to achieve a gold disc for 100,000 copies sold would be a fantastic result, but the mixture of ballads and dance tunes proved to be a perfect recipe for success.

Everything Changes
Highest UK chart position: 1
Year: 1993
Track listing/writer(s):
Everything Changes (Gary Barlow/Cary Baylis/Eliot Kennedy/Mike Ward)
Pray (Gary Barlow)

Wasting My Time (Gary Barlow)
Relight My Fire (Dan Hartman)
Love Ain't Here Anymore (Gary Barlow)
If This is Love (Howard Donald/Dave James)
Whatever You Do to Me (Gary Barlow)
Meaning of Love (Gary Barlow)
Why Can't I Wake Up with You? (Gary Barlow)
You Are the One (Gary Barlow)
Another Crack in My Heart (Gary Barlow)
Broken Your Heart (Gary Barlow)
Babe (Gary Barlow)
Producers: Paul Jervier, Steve Jervier, Eliot Kennedy, Jonathan Wales, Mike Ward
The band's second studio album picked up where its predecessor had left off, dethroning Meat Loaf's *Bat Out Of Hell II – Back Into Hell* from the top of the charts on 23 October 1993. Sadly, Take That's stay in the peak position lasted only seven days as the American gained his revenge the following week. With the album containing four Number 1 hits, it's no wonder that more than 300,000 copies flew off the shelves in the first week of release.

A more mature mix of songs, it was also notable for *If This Is Love*, which

RIGHT Take
That performing
'Shine', with Gary
at the piano

was Howard's first published foray into songwriting.

Nobody Else
Highest UK chart position: 1
Year: 1995
Track listing/writer(s):
Sure (Gary Barlow/Mark Owen/Robbie Williams)
Back for Good (Gary Barlow)
Every Guy (Gary Barlow)
Sunday to Saturday (Gary Barlow/Howard Donald/Mark Owen)
Nobody Else (Gary Barlow)
Never Forget (Gary Barlow)
Hanging Onto Your Love (Gary Barlow/David Morales)
Hate It (Gary Barlow)
Lady Tonight (Gary Barlow)
The Day After Tomorrow (Gary Barlow)
Producers: Gary Barlow, Brothers in Rhythm, David Morales, Chris Porter, Jim Steinman

Released in May 1995 – just a month after the departure of Robbie Williams – *Nobody Else* spent two weeks at Number 1 and put to rest fans' fears that Take That had nothing left to offer. The artwork and most of the recording had been completed before the group slimmed down to a foursome, so it was decided to issue it with Robbie's contributions in place.

Despite containing the Number 1 hits *Sure*, *Back For Good* and *Never Forget*, the album's sales fell short of *Everything Changes*, but it did give the band their first US chart entry, albeit at a lowly Number 69.

Beautiful World
Highest UK chart position: 1
Year: 2006
Track listing/writer(s):
Reach Out (Take That/John Shanks)
Patience (Take That/John Shanks)
Beautiful World (Take That/Steve Robson)
Hold On (Take That/John Shanks)
Like I Never Loved You at All (Take That/John Shanks)
Shine (Take That/Steve Robson)
I'd Wait for Life (Take That)
Ain't No Sense in Love (Take That/Billy Mann)
What You Believe In (Take That/Anders Bagge)
Mancunian Way (Take That/Eg White)
Wooden Boat (Take That/John Shanks)
Butterfly (hidden track) (Take That/John

RIGHT The band launching 'Beautiful World' in 2006

Shanks)

Producer: John Shanks

The first new Take That album in a decade was eagerly anticipated and, when it was released in November 2006, it didn't disappoint. *Beautiful World* was a departure from their previous offerings in that each of the four members sang lead vocals on at least one track, although Gary still claimed the lion's share of this task with six of the twelve songs. The album was extremely well received by critics and fans alike and has since sold more than 2.6 million copies in the UK alone.

The Circus

Highest UK chart position: 1
Year: 2008
Track listing/writer(s):
The Garden (Take That)
Greatest Day (Take That)
Hello (Take That/Steve Robson)
Said It All (Take That/Steve Robson)
Julie (Take That/Steve Robson)
The Circus (Take That)
How Did It Come to This (Take That/Jamie Norton/Ben Mark)
Up All Night (Take That/Jamie Norton)

What is Love (Take That)
You (Take That)
Hold Up a Light (Take That/Jamie Norton)
Here (Take That/Olly Knights/Gale Paridjanian)
She Said (hidden track) (Take That)
Producer: John Shanks
Coincidentally released at the same time as Britney Spears' album *Circus*, Take That's fifth studio offering broke the records for the number of pre-release orders, and sold 133,000 copies on the first day of sales in the UK. Needless to say, it topped the UK album charts and stayed in the Top 100 for seventy-three weeks.

The Circus, which yielded five singles, was almost universally liked by the critics and was promoted by a stadium that became the fastest-selling in UK history. It even beat sales for Michael Jackson's Bad tour in 1987.

The Greatest Day – Take That Present: The Circus Live

Highest UK chart position: 3
Year: 2009

Track listing/writer(s):
Disc one – live at Wembley
Greatest Day (Take That)
Hello (Take That/Steve Robson)
Pray (Gary Barlow)
Back for Good (Gary Barlow)
The Garden (Take That)
Shine (Take That/Steve Robson)
Up All Night (Take That/Jamie Norton)
How Did it Come to This (Take That/Jamie Norton/Ben Mark)
The Circus (Take That)
What is Love (Take That)
Said It All (Take That/Steve Robson)
Never Forget (Gary Barlow)
Patience (Take That/John Shanks)
Relight My Fire (Dan Hartman)
Hold Up a Light (Take That/Jamie Norton)
Rule the World (Take That)
Bonus disc – In session at Abbey Road
The Garden (Take That)
How Did It Come to This (Take That/Jamie Norton/Ben Mark)
Greatest Day (Take That)
Up All Night (Take That/Jamie Norton)
Patience (Take That/John Shanks)
What is Love (Take That)
The Circus (Take That)
Shine (Take That/Steve Robson)
Rule the World (Take That)
Julie (Take That/Steve Robson)
Said It All (Take That/Steve Robson)
Producer: John Shanks

Take That's first live album, recorded at London's Wembley Stadium in July 2009, has so far only been released in the UK and Ireland. The live segment was accompanied by a bonus disc containing recordings from a session at the famous Abbey Road studios. It stayed in the UK Top 100 for three months.

Progress

Highest UK chart position: 1
Year: 2010
Track listing:
All songs written by Gary Barlow, Howard Donald, Jason Orange, Mark Owen and Robbie Williams.
The Flood
SOS
Wait
Kidz
Pretty Things
Happy Now
Underground Machine
What do You Want from Me?
Affirmation
Eight Letters

Flowerbed (hidden track)
Producer: Stuart Price
Fifteen years after *Nobody Else*, the last album released by a five-piece Take That, *Progress* saw the return to the fold of Robbie Williams and sold more than 235,000 UK copies on its first day. That made it the twenty-first century's fastest-selling record.

To say that fans welcomed Robbie's return is to understate things a little The album topped the European charts as well as in individual territories like Denmark, Germany, Greece and Ireland, in addition to the UK. By April 2011, it had been certified platinum six times in the band's home country.

Progress Live
Highest UK chart position: 12
Year: 2011
Track listing/writers:
Rule the World (Take That)
Greatest Day (Take That)
Hold Up a Light (Take That/Ben Mark/Jamie Norton)
Patience (Take That/John Shanks)
Shine (Take That/Steve Robson)
Let Me Entertain You (Robbie Williams/Guy Chambers)
Rock DJ (Robbie Williams/Guy Chambers/Kelvin Andrews/Nelson Pigford/Ekundayo Paris)
Come Undone (Robbie Williams/Kristian Ottestad/Ashley Hamilton/Daniel Pierre)
Feel (Robbie Williams/Guy Chambers)
Angels (Robbie Williams/Guy Chambers)
The Flood (Take That)
SOS (Take That)
Underground Machine (Take That)
Kidz (Take That)
Pretty Things (Take That)
When They Were Young (Gary Barlow/Michael Ward/Eliot Kennedy/Cary Bayliss)
Back for Good (Gary Barlow)
Pray (Gary Barlow)
Love Love (Take That)
Never Forget (Gary Barlow)
No Regrets/Relight My Fire (Robbie Williams/Guy Chambers; Dan Hartman)
Eight Letters (Take That)
The band's second live album was made from recordings at concerts at Wembley Stadium, London and the Etihad Stadium, Manchester during the triumphant Progress tour of 2011.

**The pictures in this book were
provided courtesy of the following:**

GETTY IMAGES
101 Bayham Street, London NW1 0AG

Design and artwork by Scott Giarnese

Published by G2 Entertainment Limited

Publishers: Jules Gammond and Edward Adams

Revised by Pat Morgan